Viola Time Joggers

Viola accompaniment book

Kathy and David Blackwell

T0071020

Teacher's note

These duet parts are written to accompany the tunes in *Viola Time Joggers*. They are an alternative to the piano accompaniments or audio tracks, and are not designed to be used with those items. A separate violin duet book is available providing duet parts for when violas play together with violins using *Fiddle Time Joggers*.

Kathy and David Blackwell

OXFORD
UNIVERSITY PRESS

Great Clarendon Street, Oxford OX2 6DP, England
This collection © Oxford University Press 2005, 2013, and 2022
Unless marked otherwise, all pieces (music and words) are by Kathy and David Blackwell and are © Oxford University Press. All traditional pieces are arranged by Kathy and David Blackwell and are © Oxford University Press. Unauthorized arrangement or photocopying of this copyright material is ILLEGAL.

Kathy and David Blackwell have asserted their right under the Copyright, Designs and Patents Act, 1988, to be identified as the Composers of this Work.

Impression: 2

ISBN: 978-0-19-356214-1

Music and text origination by Katie Johnston
Printed in Great Britain on acid-free paper by
Halstan & Co. Ltd, Amersham, Bucks.

Contents

1. Bow down, O Belinda 3
2. Under arrest! 3
3. Someone plucks, someone bows 4
4. Down up 4
5. Two in a boat 5
6. London Bridge 5
7. Fast lane 6
8. In flight 7
9. Lift off! 8
10. Katie's waltz 8
11. Copy cat 9
12. Tap dancer 10
13. Rhythm fever 11
14. Here it comes! 12
15. So there! 12
16. Rowing boat 13
17. Ally bally 14
18. Tiptoe, boo! 14
19. Travellin' slow 16
20. C string boogie 16
21. Off to Paris 17
22. Clare's song 18
23. City lights 19
24. Daydream 20
25. On the prowl 21
26. Summer sun 22
27. Phoebe in her petticoat 23
28. Ready, steady, go now! 23
29. Cooking in the kitchen 24
30. Happy go lucky 24
31. The mocking bird 26
32. Algy met a bear 26
33. Listen to the rhythm 27
34. Cattle ranch blues 28
35. In the groove 29
36. Stamping dance 30
37. Distant bells 30
38. Lazy scale 31
39. Runaway train 32
40. Rocking horse 33
41. Patrick's reel 34
42. Calypso time 35
43. Tudor tune 36
44. Chopsticks for two 37
45. Carrion crow 38
46. Flying high 39
47. Viola Time 40

1. Bow down, O Belinda

American folk tune

2. Under arrest!

KB & DB

Say the word 'rest' quietly to yourself as you play.

3. Someone plucks, someone bows

Traditional
Words KB & DB

4. Down up

C string special

KB & DB

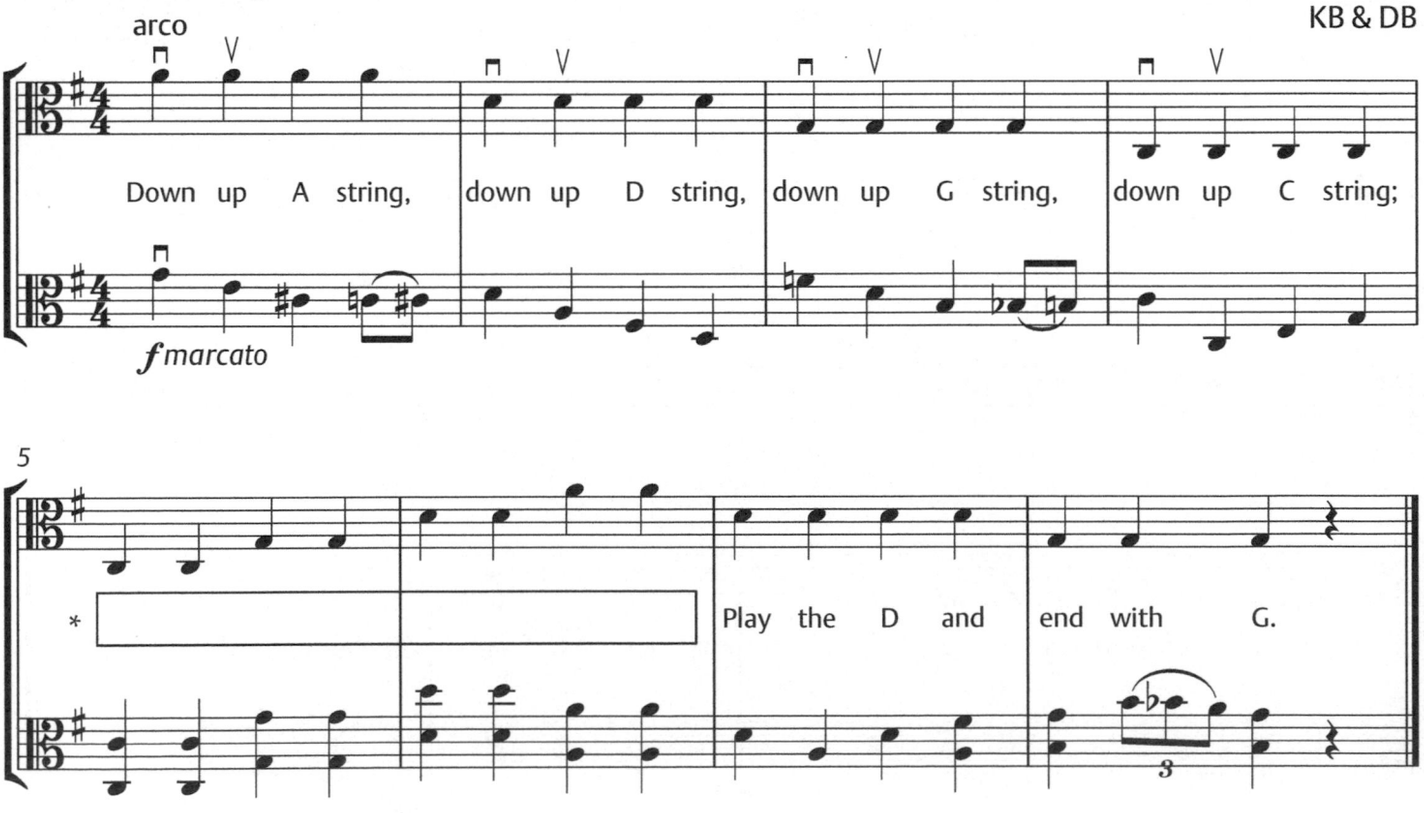

* Fill in the letter names of these notes.

5. Two in a boat

American folk tune

6. London Bridge

English folk tune

7. Fast lane

Try even faster the second time through!

8. In flight

In the rests, let your bow make a circle as you swoop and soar like a bird.

9. Lift off!

Lift your bow off in each of the rests and let it orbit! (Make a circle with your right arm.)

10. Katie's waltz

11. Copy cat

KB & DB

mf

D D E E

Can you play what I play? D D E E

5

Fine

Can you play what I play? Play it now with me.

9

A A B B

Can you play what I play? A A B B

13

D.C. al Fine

Can you play what I play? Play it now with me.

12. Tap dancer

* Hold the bow upright and tap the screw end of the bow on your music stand.

13. Rhythm fever

KB & DB

14. Here it comes!

KB & DB

* Think of a foody rhythm and play it on these notes.

15. So there!

KB & DB

16. Rowing boat

KB & DB

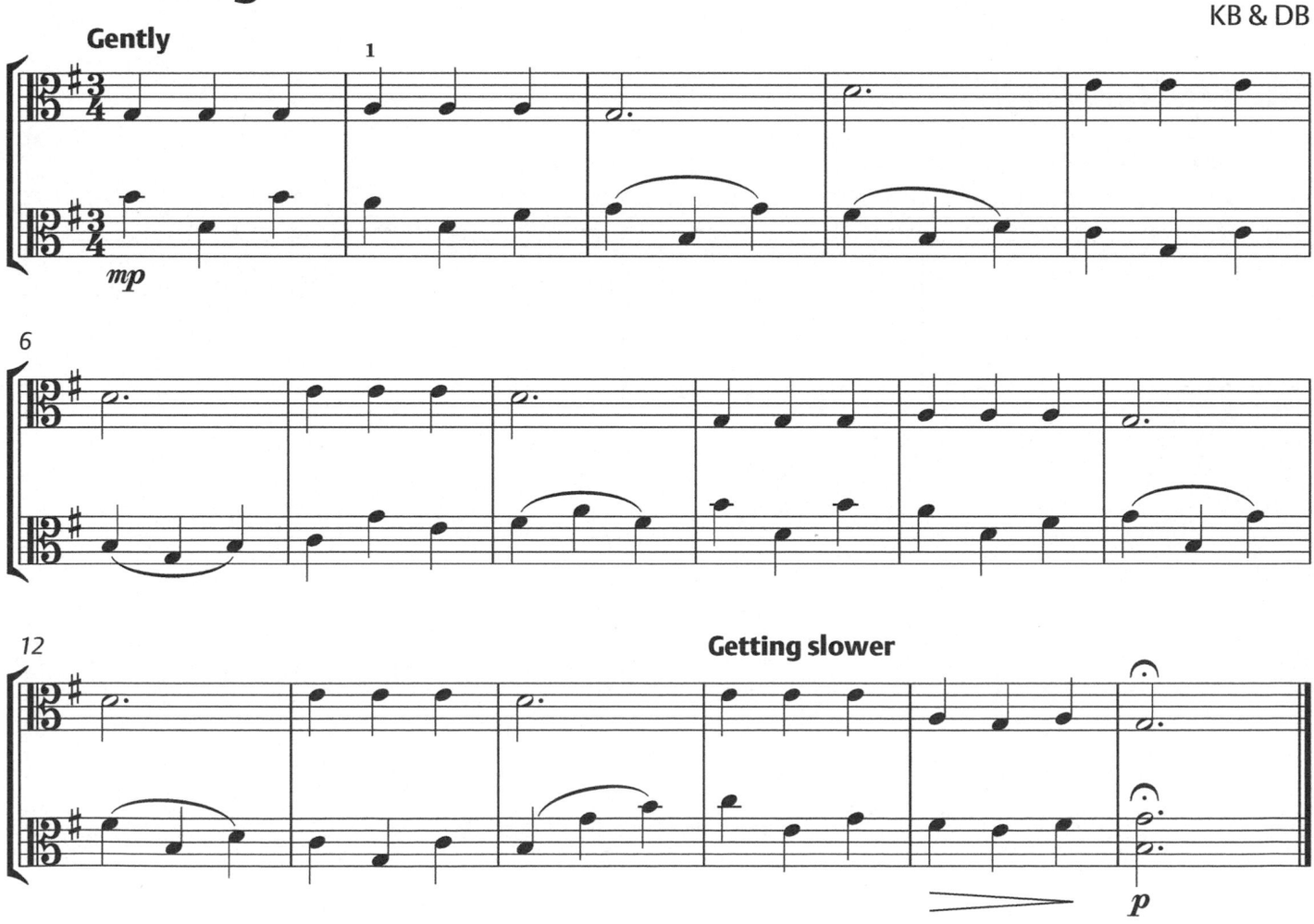

17. Ally bally

Scottish folk tune

18. Tiptoe, boo!

KB & DB

The pupil's part may also be played pizzicato.

19. Travellin' slow

KB & DB

20. C string boogie

C string special

KB & DB

* Turn around or, if you are sitting, stand up and sit down again!

21. Off to Paris

French folk tune

22. Clare's song

KB & DB

23. City lights

KB & DB

24. Daydream

C string special

KB & DB

25. On the prowl

C string special

KB & DB

26. Summer sun

KB & DB

27. Phoebe in her petticoat

American folk tune

Swap parts when you do the repeat.

28. Ready, steady, go now!

KB & DB

29. Cooking in the kitchen

KB & DB

30. Happy go lucky (for Iain)

KB & DB

13
mf
mf
19
f
f
25
31
ff
ff

31. The mocking bird

American folk tune

32. Algy met a bear

KB & DB
Words anon.

Swap parts when you do the repeat.

33. Listen to the rhythm

KB & DB

34. Cattle ranch blues

KB & DB

35. In the groove

36. Stamping dance

Czech folk tune

37. Distant bells

KB & DB

38. Lazy scale

KB & DB

39. Runaway train

C string special

KB & DB

40. Rocking horse

41. Patrick's reel

KB & DB

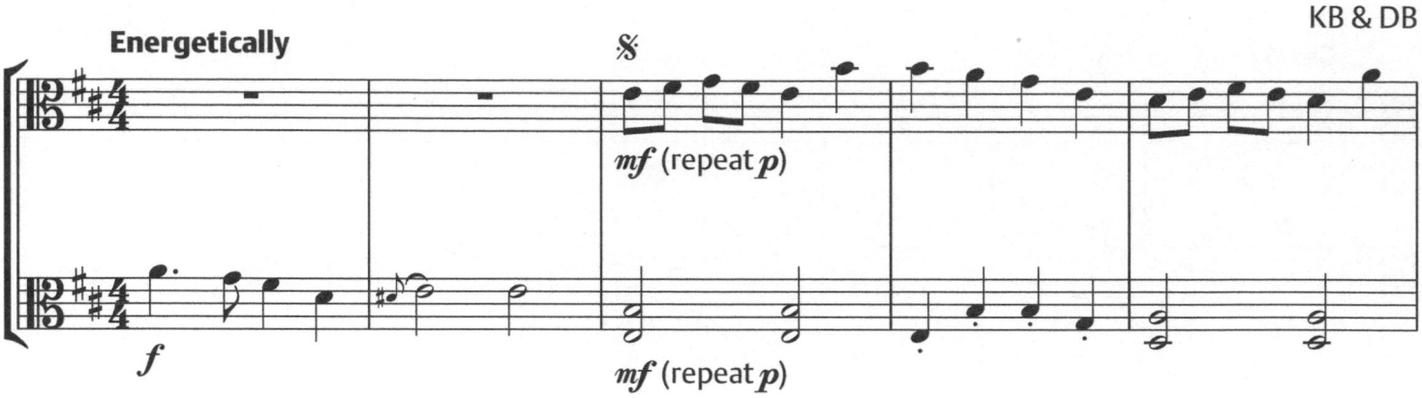

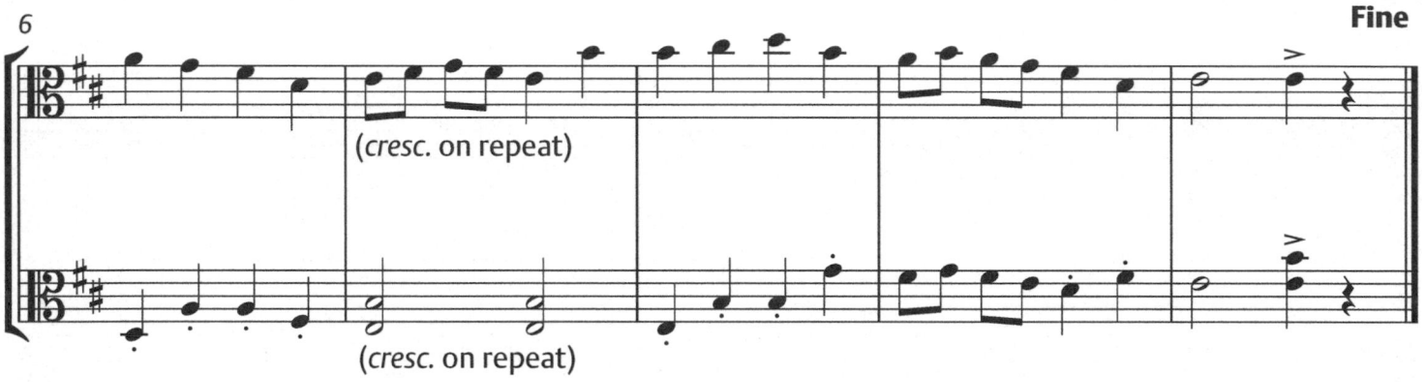

42. Calypso time

KB & DB

43. Tudor tune

C string special

KB & DB

44. Chopsticks for two

C string special

KB & DB

45. Carrion crow

American folk tune

46. Flying high

47. Viola Time